Spectrum

Hastings College
Literary and Art Magazine

Spring 2020

This magazine was made possible by funds from the Student Association. All submissions were generously shared by Hastings College students.

The publication board was selected from a group of volunteers. Submissions were chosen by tallying the scores given to works anonymously. Individuals on the publication board did not review their own works.

All final decisions regarding this publication were made by the editors.

Santa Fe

by Caitlin Smith

CONTENTS

A Note from the Editors:

Thank you for taking the time to read this issue of *Spectrum!* This publication has been a tradition on the Hastings College campus for a long time. Old issues of *Spectrum* dating back to 1926 can be found in the library. *Spectrum* is student run and consists of student work. The past few issues of *Spectrum* are available online! Visit: https://sites.google.com/hastings.edu/spectrum/home

Rose with Black
Watercolor
Sydnie Waldron

To My Future Partner

By Jordan Ismaiel

I hope you're good with power tools.
Because I'm afraid of using a drill, or a saw.
I could watch as you build a table from your hands
like making the world out of nothing.
We could eat from it while we sit on the same side,
My hand slowly making its way
Down your back as we eat dinner.
I hope you enjoy cars.
So that way you can drive whenever we go somewhere.
I wouldn't have to worry about the road as I
Rest my head against your shoulder.
My hand slowly working its way
Across your body to embrace your heat,
Because I also like having the air cold.
I hope you like movies.
That way I never go to the matinee alone,
We get the whole theater to ourselves
Like maybe nothing else matters because
The empty seats have all the other possibilities.
My hand slowly drifting to share the armrest,
just so I can hold your hand.
I hope you can carry me home.
After I hit the concrete because I fell too hard.
I blamed my lack of paying attention, but
I was actually staring at you as you looked forward,
Like you were hopeful for our future.
My hand slowly made its way around you
As you picked me up like it was everything.
I hope you're good with kids.
I convinced myself I would never
Be a good parent, or a father,
Or anything in between.
I hold our child as you say it'll be alright,
That I'm doing fine.
Your hand slowly making its way under mine,
Under our child's head. Telling me that this
Is everything you've ever wanted.

We the People
Oil on wooden panel
Jordan Ismaiel

Alternatives

By Lilly Nelms

Someone has stood where you have,
Unsure of where curiosity will take
them.

Choices.

Take a step, whatever way.

To the right a gleaming red door.
Left, a breadcrumb path. Analyze
them, what will you find?

Red door, a heavy key appears within your fists. The
breadcrumb path seems promising with the songs of birds.
Both do not unveil the unknown territory beyond Or the
consequences—

The
door.

Twist the key in the lock. Step past the
threshold To hear the boards creak. It is
empty besides your reflection In the ornate
mirror casting opposite of you. Let secrets
unfold with each step.

It is within sight, but you are not there. Instead
you find the door again, Reflecting another
opening. Shimmering surface and unbound
curiosity Brings your foot to what should have
been glass.

Go
on.

Your hand trembles upon a new handle.

Pull.

Falling—rose thorns grab and tear.
Land on your back To face the
monsters that stare. Blood and
panic arise.

Run.

Away you go. Roots trip,
Crows roar. Trees sway for
your demise.

They are
coming.

Blood pumping to no end.
Scratches red as the door
You choose to go in. Don't
look behind. Witches,
wolves, and beasts Nip at
your feet. Until his arrows
graze past, Finding their
mark.

He stands proud, Your prince flesh
and blood, Appearing in the nick of
time. Fall in love at first sight. Run
away to live happily ever after.

Choices were made Although
they could be changed. Travel to
the past.

The breadcrumb
path.

Sheltered,
Full of life.

Follow to discover a lovely cottage;
Away from all that might come near.
Step inside and hide away for a year.
Until one day, a knock at your door.

Beware.

Open to find a wrinkled soul,
Offering all that you could ever need.
Like the cottage below your feet Isn't
enough to secede that greed.

Sending her away, To her own
cottage Crumbling from age. You
didn't know How you offend her so. With a pot, And the heart of the
rarest creature, She waits for your
curse to set.

Wake
up.

Something is wrong. The air is
silent with no melodies. The trees
no longer sway. Your garden lies
in twigs.

Hungry, you see the fresh breadcrumb path.
Hoping it leads you back. Nibbling all that
follows forth to an end. The barren cottage
welcomes you from your loop.

Day after day. Cursed life to be a
continuous cycle, Crumb after
crumb. Till you question Who is the
old lady in the reflection?

Red
Photography
Caitlin Smith

Why I Write

By Rylie Felton

In 5th grade, I wrote
a fairytale. I do not remember
what it was about but
my teacher liked it so much
she made me read it
to the class. I was too quiet
so she made me stand
on a chair. My fire for writing
was ignited.

Middle school you would
most likely find me writing
during math class, scribbling
rapidly the stories that had
made a home in my head.
I got such a rush bringing
my characters to life
and taking them on adventures.

But as I looked back
at what I had created
all I could hear was "Not good
enough, not good enough."
Something new was making
it's home inside my head
and everything was getting
dark and cold. The fire
was out.

When high school came around
I was lost. I couldn't be an author
so I settled for being a therapist.
Speech was fun because I didn't
have to write anything myself, I performed
other people's stories.

Then I found slam poetry
and my whole world changed.
I memorized all the poems I could,
but I could never write my own.
Not good enough, not good enough.

It only took some trauma and
abandonment for me to not care
what my head told me and take
a leap. And I would never regret
that leap into slam camp.
I was surrounded by poets like me
who wanted to learn and grow
to not be judged or mocked.
We were all there for each other.
I found a community I had been
missing. My fire was higher
than ever. They inspire me.

In my senior year I took a creative
writing class. My old school didn't
offer anything even similar to it.
We made commercials, wrote poems,
and a 10-page short story. My teacher
wrote on mine, "Never stop
writing!"

Maybe I do it for the attention.
Or because I want to be famous.
I want to sell books as popular
as Rupi Kar
Maybe I do it because
it makes me happy.
Or because it's cool.
Or because someone else can relate
to how I'm feeling.
Or because I am trying to make people
feel what I feel.
Maybe I do it
to feel less
alone.

Glass Roses
Glass
Christian Hessler

Bottle Vision
Photography
Sage Reiger

Who Am I?

By Lyette Erin

I was a lignum vitae
But I have lost everything.

If I were a hibiscus,
would you abandon me like a
maligned potcake?

I have lost my blossoms,
Trunk has been severed,
Roots have been deracinated.

If I were a yellow elder
would my sunshine
petals bewitch you to gaze upon
my beauty?

Without my leaves,
How will you know
that I was a medicinal
wood of life?

If I were a bougainvillea painted
in your favourite colour,
would you uproot me,
and arrange me proudly in
your home?

Without my trunk,
How will you know
that I have survived
thousands of hurricanes?

If I were a bird of paradise
pungent and vibrant
and you plucked me...
my sharp petals would slice your flesh.

Without my roots,
How will I regrow?

Hands
Acrylic
Karlie Norton

Shallow Waters

By Abigail Shaw

There is a beauty to the
shallows,

which slowly seeps into the surrounding earth
much like a spilled latte
soaks into a napkin
splotching the ink,
his name now
unrecognizable.

The memory of his smile
now soiled but always returning,
much like the tide.

Saturday morning
she searches for his scent
in a sea of sheets
to the steady
drip
of
her
coffee maker.

The want for safety too slight
when compared to her need for a connection
both sacred and sensual,

a love too shallow
for her to sink.

Jelly Beans
Mixed Media
Melissa Loney

Henry
Acrylic
Neely Tubbs

Apathetic

By Lyette Erin

Do not say that I do not feel
Like a statue of cold marble,
Devoid of flesh and blood, surreal;
Do not say that I do not feel

My emotions are stronger than you think
Though my words of it are but few,
It is a thread that has been interlinked,
My love is stronger than you think;

Or that I am not perfection's seal;
For your truth is entirely garbled;
Do not say that I do not feel
Like a statue of cold marble.

Many are the reasons our experiences link
What you feel, I have felt too
My emotions are stronger than you think,
Though, my words of it are but few.

Tie Dye
Mixed Media
Melissa Loney

The Partridge

By Kenzie Kolle

The man stood before the mirror—cracked and covered in years of grime—a frail, sickly specter. Once he was a handsome, brilliant young inventor now he was simply the shadow of an old, hopeless man. If you could still call him a 'man'.

His face was once strikingly handsome. Now, pale, papery skin drooped as if melting from his skull, dry and freckled with liver spots. Wrinkles carved deep crevices around his eyes, forehead and mouth. Not lines caused by cheer and happiness but lines from decades—what felt like centuries—of despair and loneliness. A beard, grey, scraggly, and unkempt, hung limply from his once strong, cutting jaw and three silver hairs swept across his ashy scalp.

His body, once strong and sturdy, was like that of a walking skeleton. Thin, ghostly white skin, mapped with the haunting blue of his veins and luminous white lesions wrapped around his aching, grinding, creaking bones. Hunched over to lean on a thick wooden cane, clutching it with knobby, claw-like fingers.

His eyes, good gods, his eyes. They were hollow. Devoid of the spark of life he had in his youth. When one looked into those eyes it was like staring into the pit of Tartarus itself. Blacker than black could be described and as cold as Cocytus, the frozen river of Hell.

However, the worst feature of this man stayed barely hidden behind the threadbare cloth of his shirt—once white, but now a dusty gray, stained with sweat and grease.

A brand.

Located directly over his heart. A grotesque, twisted plot of fried skin in the shape of a small bird. Still as hot, and red, and bubbly as the day it was given. Never healing and always burning.

It was almost like a living, sentient thing. Sometimes, the man could almost manage to disregard the pain of the mark. But as if sensing it was being ignored, the disgusting stamp would flare up, searing the man until he was on his knees, gasping for breath and begging for mercy.

The brand of the partridge, given to him by the goddess Athena, was a reminder of his sins.

His calls for leniency were never met with pity from the goddess, only disdain. For she had her reasons for bestowing this curse upon him, he knew that now.

Long ago, the young boy, Perdix, his own nephew, had come to work as the man's apprentice. And the boy was a genius, truly brilliant. Far smarter than the man and growing more so everyday. He knew this. Watched as the boy built revolutionary gadgets everyday as if they were nothing. Like he hadn't just changed the world.

Thus the man's fatal flaw was revealed to the world: Envy. The green eyed monster.

Who did this child—this young upstart—think he is. Does he think himself better than me.

So he killed young Perdix. He pushed him from a mountain without a second's hesitation. He claimed to the villagers that the boy had simply fallen. Of course, the gods are not so easily fooled.

Athena came to him that night in his dreams. She admonished the man for his envy, his lack of morality and swore he would pay greatly for his crimes. The man awoke violently to white-hot, volcanic heat on his chest. Pain wracked his body like his skin was being ripped from his bones as the brand was given. He would never forget the smell of his own flesh baking and the sonorous sound of the goddesses voice echoing in his cranium before he lost consciousness.

Now, he is cursed for his jealousy. Cursed to wander this plane alone, penniless. Forced to carry the burden of his sins for the rest of his pathetic excuse of a life.

The man turned away from the mirror, disgusted. A single oil lamp sat on a stump in the corner of his room. Its dying flame illuminated the tiny space, casting ominous shadows on the barren, rickety walls. Exhausted, the man lay on the sack of hay that passed for his bed. Closing his lifeless eyes, he wished for peace as the darkness enveloped him.

But he knew he would never be at peace. For when his soul descends to the realm of Hades, then will his suffering truly begin.

He could almost hear the damned calling for him.

Daedalus.

Daedalus.

Daedalus.

www.ingramcontent.com/pod-product-compliance
Lightning Source LLC
Chambersburg PA
CBHW042109160726
48295CB00017B/1040

* 9 7 8 1 9 4 2 8 8 5 7 8 8 *